MY FIRST TRIP TO THE POST OFFICE/ MI PRIMERA VISITA AL CORREO

By Katie Kawa   Traducción al español: Eduardo Alamán

Gareth Stevens
Publishing

Please visit our website, www.garethstevens.com. For a free color catalog of all our high-quality books, call toll free 1-800-542-2595 or fax 1-877-542-2596.

Library of Congress Cataloging-in-Publication Data

Kawa, Katie.
[My first trip to the post office. Spanish & English]
My first trip to the post office = Mi primera visita al correo / Katie Kawa.
    p. cm. — (My first adventures = Mis primeras aventuras)
In English and Spanish.
Includes index.
ISBN 978-1-4339-6633-0 (library binding)
1. Postal service. I. Title. II. Title: Mi primera visita al correo.
HE6078.K393 2012
383'.42—dc23

                            2011031671

First Edition

Published in 2012 by
Gareth Stevens Publishing
111 East 14th Street, Suite 349
New York, NY 10003

Copyright © 2012 Gareth Stevens Publishing

Editor: Katie Kawa
Designer: Haley W. Harasymiw
Spanish Translation: Eduardo Alamán

All illustrations by Planman Technologies

Printed in the United States of America

CPSIA compliance information: Batch #CW12GS: For further information contact Gareth Stevens, New York, New York at 1-800-542-2595.

Contents

Sending a Letter 4

What Is a Stamp? .16

Special Delivery! .20

Words to Know 24

Index 24

- -

Contenido

Enviando una carta 4

¿Qué es una estampilla? 16

¡Entrega especial! .20

Palabras que debes saber 24

Índice 24

I love to get mail!

¡Me encanta recibir correo!

5

I wrote a letter
to my Aunt Amy.
She lives far away.

Le escribo una carta
a mi tía Amy.
Mi tía vive lejos.

I am taking it to
the post office.

Llevo la carta al correo.

This is a place
to send mail.

Este es un lugar para
enviar cartas.

My mom and I wait in line.
Then, a man helps us.

Espero en fila con mi mamá.
Un hombre nos ayuda.

He is a postal worker.

Él es un empleado postal.

My mom buys stamps.
They look like stickers.

Mi mamá compra
estampillas. Las estampillas
son como pegatinas.

Every letter needs a stamp.
I stick one on mine.

Cada carta necesita
estampillas. Yo pongo
una en mi carta.

18

I give my letter
to the worker.
Soon, it will go
on a mail truck.

Se la doy al empleado
postal. Pronto, mi carta
se irá en una camioneta
de correo.

21

Then, Aunt Amy will get my letter!

¡Luego, mi tía Amy recibirá mi carta!

23

Words to Know/
Palabras que debes saber

letter/
(la) carta

postal worker/
(el/la) empleado(a)
postal

stamp/
(la) estampilla

Index / Índice

letter/(la) carta 6, 8,
    10, 18, 20, 22

mail/correo 4, 10, 20

postal worker/(el/la)
    empleado(a) postal 14,
    20

stamp/(la) estampilla 16, 18